Dear Joan

Thanks for the fine

communication.

Geert

JOKERMAN

HAIBUN ABOUT PLAYING CARDS
GEERT VERBEKE

JOKERMAN © Cyberwit.net & Geert Verbeke.
4/2 B, L.I.G.
Govindpur Colony,
Allahabad-211004 (U.P) India
Tel: 91-532-2541153
E-mail: cyberwit@rediffmail.com
www.cyberwit.net

ISBN: 81-8253-038-5
First Edition: 2005
Rs. 100/-

© JOKERMAN:
Geert Verbeke
14 Leo Baekelandlaan
8500 Kortrijk
Flanders – Belgium – Europe
Tel: 0032.56.21.88.25

Communication: haikugeert@hotmail.com
Website: http://users.skynet.be/geert.verbeke.bowls

JOKERMAN
GEERT VERBEKE

Any paranormal power regarding the cards aside, I am intrigued by their use to provide new perspectives to events in our lives. Geert's loving fascination with playing cards comes out with his vibrant descriptions and accounts which made me appreciate the art and symbolism in their printings that before I had taken for granted. His inclusion here of their history and cultural influences is enlightening. Geert's haiku poetry is powerful and his prose flows like poetic free verse peppered with images from a world traveler, his wonderful humor and personal insights.

Poet Michael Baribeau, Michigan, USA.

3

ACKNOWLEDGEMENTS:

This modest book, 'Jokerman' only exists for a part as a product of the communication with generous friends and fellow aficionados who inspired me with their love, generous advice & comments on the text. From all of them, I had much to learn! For each I have a unique feeling of gratitude & a warm appreciation. Thank you dear Jenny Ovaere, Marc Awodey, Michael Baribeau, Jane Reichhold & Henk Werkhoven for the first readings of 'Jokerman', your observations have been important to give good shape to this book.

DEDICATED TO:

Jenny Ovaere, I love you'cause you're wise.
My peculiar kids: Hans, Saskia, Merlijn & Jonas.
Tine Beeckmans, Susie Colman & Rita Verhoeven my lady friends.
Roland Delaere for being a good Jokerman.
A lot of kuyu, my worldwide haiku friends.
Stephan Micus for music.
Woody Allen for films.
Madame Lenormand.

IN MEMORY OF:

My parents Walter Verbeke & Jo Hiltrop.
Pietro Bares, Claire Buysschaert, Barbara Kluft, Winand Fadeux & Nantes...

WARNING: this book dares to tell the truth...

JOKERMAN:

First thing first: this haibun-book is not a fortune-telling book, and certainly not the prayer book of the devil! No, this book is only written to have a good time.

The haiku is a Japanese verse form that relies on brevity and simplicity to convey its poetical message. It developed from tanka and was mainly influenced by Matsuo Bashō (1644-1694) who is known as the first great haiku poet. Indeed. a 'modern' haiku can be any length from a few to 17 syllables in 3 lines. The theme of a haiku refers to nature although 'nature' can be interpreted in a global sense. A seasonal word (kigo) is no longer a necessity.

loud swearings
after benting a nail
the carpenter

Haibun is a combination of prose and a few haiku poems. Its focus is often on everyday experiences. The haibun draws inspiration from the haiku. A well balanced haiku pays attention to daily events connected with the author, his environment and his acquaintances. The haibun asks austerity and a light-footed approach. The haiku, written with a beginner's mind in or after the haibun is a supplement to the text, not a repetition. The relationship between the prose and the haiku is often subtle. Free associations and a mild touch of irony are always present. The haibun can be written as a playful column, not necessarily following any tradition. A few authors are writing rather provocative, the haibun as a satirical blow-up.

on her table
a bouquet of lilacs
withered

You will find haibun in a bantering tone. Do you care for meditative and contemplative points of view in which humour is not overlooked? You will find your little piece of candy! The reflections are talking with a humble opinion, loving our wonderful world. All kinds of characteristics, information and playful observations are reviewed to please you, and even to badger you for a sound mind in a sound body. You're welcome.

This modest book holds up a mirror in which you and I can read a vague description of our life(s) and vitality, dignity and wisdom, love and affections, intelligence and inspiration. The most reliable results are said to be obtained by a light-hearted approach.
Haibun as a literary form is in transition, developing between spiritual meditation and playful poetry. The variety and pliability of this form makes it one of the most exciting in the haiku repertoire.

Keep away from some fortune-tellers for manipulation, cheap swindle and exorbitant prices!

ABRACADABRA
ABRACADABR
ABRACADAB
ABRACADA
ABRACAD
ABRACA
ABRAC
ABRA
ABR
AB
A

The research for profound information, meanings and associations learned that contumacy is a household word for telling fortunes with ordinary playing-cards. It is a well-known and famous form of divination that has been around for almost as long as the cards themselves. Playing-cards are in existence since thousands of years... they are a beautiful part of our entail. Their meaning, sense and symbolism has an archetypical form and content which is extraordinary, fascinating and attractive. It can't be denied that the value for relaxation and recreation of the cards is great, they are an unrivalled remedy as means of passing the time. Not only in a countless club of card players, but also in canteens and for an enjoyable time at home.

solace yourself
plonk out a song
in a piano solo

Ok, we all know that playing cards go together with gamblers, addiction and crime, but it is a fact that playing 'solitaire' (card games for one player are called 'Patience' in Britain and 'Solitaire' in the USA,) is a lifesaver for a lot of lonely people like haiku writers.

one year later
she still plays solitaire
the widow

No other pastime has exercised such a deep fascination over the mind of men as card playing and haiku writing. In general, you can't fool the votary of playing cards, and particularly not the collectors of jokers. The symbolism of hearts, diamonds, spades and clubs is: curious, odd, peculiar, weird and wonderful. Make your choice! The cards are talking about: occult wisdom from ancient civilizations, old gypsy secrets or pure magic. Playing cards, whatever their origin is, can be connected with spirituality and consciousness. Cards are linked with a wide-ranging old tradition. Is the symbolic essence originating from a mystery school, a religion or with the visionary trance of a póet, priest or shaman?

real new age
a money-making mind
and god on his side

GEERT VERBEKE
Springtime 2005

7

Jokerman dance to the nightingale tune...
Bob Dylan (Infidels - 1983)

Well take your local joker and teach him how to act...
Bruce Springsteen (For You - 1973)

THE ORIGINS:

It is only in recent decades that clues about the origins of the playing cards have begun to be understood. According to reports the earliest authentic references to playing-cards in Europe date from 1377. But jokers adore the fool's dress, so they are whispering: 'Cards must have been invented in China, where paper was invented, or in India, Persia and maybe the lost civilization of Mu.' Or was Atlantis the cradle of the cards?

The French occultist Court de Gebelin asked in the eighteenth century if the tree of knowledge, about cards, was growing in Egypt or in Chaldea? An other French occultist Eteilla (1738-1791) (pseudonym for Jean-Baptiste Alliette), who played early on a central role in the development of the Tarot, was wondering if the playing cards originated from the book of Toth, or even from a book of Hermes Trismegistos saved from the burnt down Alexandrine library.

in the shadow
of the scarecrow
a devil's claw

The cards are shrouded in mysteries. Are they messengers? Or a quest for modern mankind, on the road with new visions about our place and meaning in the cosmos? There are a lot of assumptions and remarkable hypothesis, giving some light on the matter and evoking new questions. It is likely that the cards (Latin = charta, what means: paper) are connected with Arabia, with the so called Mameluk-cards rooted in the fifteenth century. There is also an Egyptian card-fragment, of the twelfth century, with four series of coins, cups, batons and swords. Cartomancy is the word for telling fortunes with ordinary playing cards but you would be well-advised to consult the Internet, if you like to get the hang and the development of fortune telling.

fortune telling
and an exorbitant price
dim the light

You may keep what you find? The immediate causes for writing this book are my mad love for haiku and my retrieval of lost playing cards on trains, airports, Chinese restaurants, busy crossing, bus shelters and all kind of other public places. Searching a long time now, I have found more then 600 playing cards. Between tombstones near the fishing port of Mahdia, between souks and medinas, dozens of examples on the road between El-Djem and Kairouan in Tunisia, in my own town Kortrijk, the Great Place of Brussels, the beach at Ostend, the Zoo at Antwerp, near the Eiffeltower at Paris.

synagogue
on Desolation Day
he clears snow

For me, playing cards are always around somewhere, even lengthwise torn in two: in the shadow of the Great mosque in Caïro, on the marked place of Zanzibar City, in a small village in Tanzania, in my hotel in Sousse, Tunisia. I always picked them up, literally out of the gutter. Sometimes the same card: a half Six of Hearts. Synchronism with a secret meaning, hidden wisdom or by chance? By coincidence? A crystal-gazer told me: 'Soon, you are going to get what you want! Good luck is coming your way. Someone is taking warm interest in you. The Six of Hearts indicates for you a charming surprise!'

sunbather
on his ass
a starfish

Fascinating and lucky strikes, in the presence of witnesses. Meaningful with reference to people, major events and encounters. The playing cards are signposts. Prudence is called for, most certainly if the interpretations are too rigid. The blunders always exist, notwithstanding the fact that the hidden messages of colours and illustrations never escape the scrutinizing look of the wise mind. Our playful mind considers the playing cards as stimulants for the imagination and our expressive capacities, as reminders oriented towards new reasoning. An old Hindu-story tells us that a loving and affectionate wife invented the playing cards to cure her consort, a mighty Maharaja, from a nervous tic, scratching his beard. Other sources are talking about gypsies and seaman. Some people make mention of extraterrestrials. E.T. phones home?

in the medina
a stall with playing cards
your warm laughter

Let the playing cards speak for themselves, while you dally with the idea of positive and negative connotations. There is truth and falsehood, wisdom and delusion in every card. Discover the veiled language, a shroud of mystery hangs over the cards. Neither believe nor reject blindly, just follow your intuition: not one playing card is right, not one playing card is wrong. Two poles are present in the playing cards: male and female, yin and yang. Unlike poles attract! Give yourself the room for personal examination. Every reflection can be a mirror image of your deeper self, your inner light. Don't use this book to take heavy-handed measures, respect the playful mind. It is a vivacious book of references. It is not intended to hurt feelings or to use as an executioner. Handle it with care. You have all the trump cards in your hand.

card playing
the taste of mango
on her lips

JOKERMAN

When the abbot plays the cards, the monks trumps!
Anonymus

Do not practise divination or sorcery.
Leviticus 19:61

Don't you think the joker laughs at you?
The Beatles

The joker then replied:
Its seems to me you learned it on the way.
Mike Batt

SYMBOLS:

Traditionally the most important symbols form a visual shorthand for ideas, functions, meanings and (religious and spiritual) customs. For thousands of years, symbols have enabled many artists, priests and craftsmen to embody their beliefs and feelings in powerful images and mysterious signs. There is a great deal of symbolism connected with the numerals, not all of it understood, because they have many links with the traditions of the hermetic Jewish Cabbala and numerology. Indeed, numbers control all our lives... but you are the number one! In old Europe (for peace) the well-known suits of Hearts (representing the church), Spades (representing the aristocracy), Diamonds (representing the soldiers) and Clubs (representing the peasants) give way to quite different sets of symbols and illustrations.

Spain and Italy show the oldest symbols: Coins, Cups, Batons and Swords. Germany shows: Hearts, Leaves, Bells (round hawkbells) and Acorns. In the Netherlands and Flanders, the acorn is a glans (penis), so in the rather sanctimonious fifteenth century there was chosen for the French symbols: Hearts, Diamonds, Spades and Clubs. They are testifying a wonderful symbolism of ancient wisdom. Playing cards are always interpreted according to the suits and values, but that doesn't means that you must pin yourself down to an interpretation. Let the cards be your inspiration, because this modest book does not say anything new in intellectual terms...

You hold the winning cards! Consider this book as an invitation to enrichment. Do not forget your sense of humour. Hilarity, a bit of teasing and amusement are guarantee.

in the ice bucket
a few playing cards
heavy petting

HEARTS:

Element: water.
Season: spring.
Symbol: love, truth & friendship, pain and suffering.
Tarot: chalices, cups & beakers.
Source: emotion, passion & compassion & romantic.

Fertility, fruitfulness and the whole state of mind are connected with this symbol. Hearts represent the forces of nature, the growth potential and adulthood. It is the symbolic source of all our affections (love, compassion, charity, joy and sorrow) and the symbol of spiritual illumination, intelligence, social and moral courage, conscience, transcendent wisdom and truth. The 'Holy Heart' says simply what it means: the divine. The liquid and melting together go hand in hand. Reacting infallibly is a striking quality. An unfavourable judgment says that hearts go together with possessive persons, suffocating love, self-pity and sentimental stuff as tear-jerkers. The cup or goblet, is a symbol of the heart in Islamic, Egyptian and Celtic traditions. Hence cups are the forerunners of the hearts suit in Tarot. The singing bowl is related to the cup, and he is also a symbol of the heart and in this sense linked with the Holy Grail. Intuition is a function of the heart. Feel the heart's connection with others. Emotional approach and passion are at the centre. The 'liquid condition' and 'melting together' are one. Finding the way back unerringly is an outstanding characteristic. An unfavourable judgment says that Hearts are linked with possessive and suffocating love, flamboyant melancholy, self-pity and sentimental tomfoolery.

rocking swing
the wind is changing
spring day

14

SPADES:

Element: fire.
Season: autumn.
Symbol: reason & justice, warnings.
Tarot: swords.
Source: thinking, justice and a rational mind.

Symbol of reason and rationality. Hard working, deduction and thinking analytically goes together to lift up the social status as the centre of interest. Analysis, judgment and catalogue are guide lines. Brains that know how to achieve a synthesis to mastermind a project are important, because knowledge and acquaintance lend space. Communication is important, the Gemini amongst us knows all about it.

Spades represent the autumn. An unfavourable judgment says that spades are the mirror image of hesitation and doubt. Provocative pronouncements and a capricious nature masks sometimes sly opportunism.

he blows mandalas
in the fallen leaves
the gusty wind

DIAMONDS:

Element: earth.
Season: summer.
Symbol: sensory perceptions, difficulties.
Tarot: pentangles or pentacles
Source: good health, impressions and sense of reality.

The business world can face the future with confidence if mental balance and efficiency is present. The material world is the main point. Patience, energy and forgiveness coincides. Reliability is an excellent quality. Diamonds represent the summer and the illumination. An unfavourable judgment says that diamonds could be scary and very possessive. Doom-mongering, defeatism and melancholy put a damper on uninhibited joy.

> *mosquitoes*
> *on a Buddha head*
> *zen-garden*

CLUBS:

Element: air.
Season: winter.
Symbol: spirit, freedom, friends, relationships.
Tarot: sticks and wands.
Source: enthusiasm & self-confidence.

Don't forget the inner world, the most important has to come first with mental and ethical activities. Youth and family ties are important in making friends. Of course, whatever we do is the expression of our true nature. Be good-humoured and confident, intuition is one of your important factors to obtain inner calm comparable to the nature of Buddha. An unfavourable judgment says that clubs can be very arrogant and self-satisfied. A misplaced sense of superiority cause frictions and bickering. Clubs are a double-edged sword, so mind what you're doing. The Club is also a Celtic symbol of divine force and the attribute of the supreme god Dagda, whose club could take or restore life.

a garden gnome
under the snowmound
still smiling

MARKS:

Comparable with the traditions of the Cabbala, cartomancy learns that the odd numbers have more harmonizing power then the even numbers. Conversely, you can also say that the even numbers are more powerful... the good old 'new' age is a bundle of contradictions. In ancient beliefs, cards are guides or messengers of the spirit world. The marks and pictures on the cards can be used as doorways to a deeper understanding of ourselves. They can be instruments and helpful tools to growth, to bring a kind of Buddhahood into 'our' world, to create a bridge to fall more and more in harmony.

Pythagoras (580-500 before Chr.) said: 'All things are numbers.' In the meantime we know that numbers are the cryptic keys to get to the bottom of the mysteries of the cosmic harmony and the whole universe. At first sight playing cards are only simple tools for pleasure, but gain more in-depth knowledge about numbers and symbols and they are astounding.

1: Ace
Represents the beginning, primordial unity and the origin of life. This number is connected with the sun and phallic and axial symbols. Lucky stones are topaz and amber. The lone wolf, or the individual, goes through unique situations and takes his decisions autonomous, he has great leadership qualities. One is the loneliness.

2
Represents the moon and the 'feminine' powers. More concerned with thought than real action. Castor and Pollux, Romulus and Remus. The pair or the yin-yang, are looking to achieve a synthesis. Cooperation is vivacious when communication and good teamwork goes together. Conflicting interests force choices to be made. The stones are jade, pearl and moonstone.

3
Represents growth and astrality, synthesis and reunion. Nimble but insecure, the three expresses himself in a flood of words.

18

Negotiating and nervousness alternate. Three is creative with Jupiter as a guiding planet. The number of harmony for Pythagoras. Amethyst is the stone of the three, what means that his colours are violet, mauve and purple.

4

Represents constructive criticism, the intellect, and from time to time a rebelliousness vision. Smart. Four is a complete number, representing the seasons and the points of the compass. Four straight lines and four right angles choose for construction. Matter and spirit melt together. Protection and brotherhood refers to the inner temple. Sapphire is the preferred stone.

5

The human number. Represents the pentangle, symbolized by Mercury, and the five senses. In spite of doubt and restlessness, with repeatedly moving from a village to the capital and back. Change of scenery and inner peace can go hand in hand. Diamonds are forever!

6

Represents the number of union, the Greek symbol of the andogyne and the whole scale of emotions (Venus). Love you. The represented love is romantic. Desire, symmetry and pure love ask experience and watchfulness. Experience of life assign authority to the world. Lucky stones are: turquoise and emerald. Let the roses bloom.

7

Represents progress. Generally thought as the holy and magical number: the seven days of creation, the seven days of the week, the seven notes of the musical scale, the seven colours of the spectrum and the rainbow, the seven virtues, the seven sacraments, the seven fixed stars, the seven graces, the seven dwarfs of Snow White, the seven gaps of the body and so on. The seven is regarded in many cultures as highly spiritual and philosophical. Seven is connected with water, especially with the sea and the oceans. Moss-agate is the lucky stone.

8

The eight or octagon represents power, mystery and sometimes contradiction. His symbol is the eternal loop. Power, property and organizational skills are important for this (un)lucky number governed by Saturn. Spatially an emblem of cosmic balance and beauty. Hindu, Celtic and other iconographic wheels are eight-armed.

9

Represents fulfillment and discharge. Passion and compassion channel the force of the foregoing numbers. The nine is as sacred as seven. In the numerology the nine is the ultimate: when multiplied by any other number it reproduces itself (eg 99 x 9= 891, then 8+9+1= 18, then 1+8= 9). Nine refers to Biblical connections (nine orders of angels), to pregnancy (nine months) and to the ancient cosmology (nine spheres).

10

Represents power of expression and the birth of results and fortune (good or bad). The finest jewel in the crown of success. The symbol of marriage in China.

THE COURT (OR FACE) CARDS:

JOKERMAN:

A foolproof joker does a somersault and moves as a playful and dancing fool between wisdom and idiocy. Let's dance the twist? No, this central figure or playful man, is not stupid or banal. Who can unite the pilgrim and the hermit in one person, provides evidence to the contrary? A jokerman is not in desperate need of a good brain in working order. A joker is a joker. Janus (Jonas?) with the many faces whistles in all candour a tune and laughs: 'Pleasure before business. Moment after moment.'
Being wrong-footed by a joker is one of the many possibilities of life. Take humour serious! The fool on the hill is alive and kicking with qualities such as: openness, independence and creativity. It's been handed down by centuries of tradition: the joker is a mirror. See the joker is a signpost of soft guidance and warm encouragement. The joker is a beacon of warning!

the joker
takes humour serious
as a wise fool

JACK OR VALET:

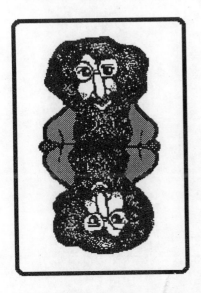

Every Jack has his Jill. Every Geert his Jenny? This is a card with an important message: 'The simple young Jack has contact with 'mother earth' and all here fruits.' The Jack, a real troublemaker according to slanderers and a misunderstood talent according to a few rare admirers gives not only evidence of self-confidence, but also a respectable portion of yin-yang and Mercurial-energies. Observer and messenger go together with his playful mind. An outstanding example of provocative mastermind or just a quite simple man? This card remind us that 'magical mystery tours' still exist. Creative thinking and opportunity scouting are outstanding tools to explore the whole wide world. No wonder that the four Jacks refers to: a sales representative, a journalist, a copywriter and an author. But cards make no claim to be exhaustive... Imagine... Lahire de Vignolles is the Valet of Heart, Ogier is the Valet of Spades, Hector (the Trojan hero) the Valet of Diamonds, and Lancelot (the Arthurian hero) the Valet of Clubs.

don't press him
sitting on a swing
with a hangover

QUEEN:

The greek goddess Pallas Athena is the Queen of Spades, Judith (the heroine of Bethulia) is the Queen of Hearts, Rachel (the biblical character) is the Queen of Diamonds, and Argine (anagram of Regina) the Queen of Clubs. God Save the Queen? Courtly love is highly recommended. This is the Mother-goddess, the generous donor of life, fertile and royal. This card reflects the ideas of sensitivity and female power. This mysterious woman, a lady to the very tips of her fingers, knows the secrets of seductive love.

She is an advisory vote and an intrigante, but she knows how to act as a mediator, especially when Peace asks to settle a dispute. This card reminds of woman's intuition, charm and wisdom. The queen is a fair-hearted woman, affectionate and faithful. The belle of the ball. Feminine power is connected with the moon. The feminine side of every man (and men) needs to be in communication with this incredible companion.

painted
on her folding fan
another fan

KING:

The symbol of absolute temporal authority. King Arthur is not far away, as a symbol of fecundity, wisdom, success and divine favour. Since ancient times, the father and the son are united in the King, who is the symbol of fatherhood, leadership and success. Mostly intelligence is dominating emotion, when the sun speaks, until the macho forget his poker face and come to recognize the necessity of an open mind and heart. Macho for the outside world, vulnerable to the confidants. His sceptre and crown witnesses of magical knowledge. Every man is a King, but I am a Flemish republican. The biblical David is the King of Spades, Alexander the Great the King of Clubs, Charles the Great (Charlemagne) the King of Hearts, and Julius Caesar the King of Diamonds.

nutty dryness
his smooth single malt
after the burial

FORTUNE FAVERS FOOLS...

THE MEANING OF THE PLAYING CARDS:

HEARTS:

Ace:	Represent a visit or a change of address.
2:	Success, often beyond expectations.
3:	An unwise or hasty decision.
4:	The bachelor or old maid card.
5:	Indecisiveness.
6:	Warning card against exploitation.
7:	A card of disappointment.
8:	A is being planned
9:	Harmony. Often called the Wish Card.
10:	A good card: means good luck.
Jack:	Help from a friend or someone close.
Queen:	A trusted woman, fair and faithful.
King:	An influential man, doing something good.

a good game
behind her cards
a broad smile

SPADES:

Ace:	Bad news about someone close.
2:	Sudden change of location or relationship.
3:	Misfortune in love or marriage.
4:	Minor misfortune, maybe a temporary setback.
5:	Success in business or love.
6:	Hard working, without much profit.
7:	Avoid arguments with friends.
8:	False friends, maybe someone will betray you.
9:	Defeat, lack of success:
10:	An unlucky card.
Jack:	He takes and takes, but does not give back.
Queen:	A cruel woman, one who interferes.
King:	One who divides and conquer.

crumpled up
under the gaming table
a trump card

DIAMONDS

Ace:	an important message, letter or gift.
2:	A serious love affair, resulting in a marriage.
3:	A card of disputes and quarrels.
4:	Quarrel between friends and family.
5:	Prosperity, long enduring friendship.
6:	An early marriage.
7:	Bad luck for a gambler or drinker.
8:	Your life is too hectic at the moment.
9:	Adventure or a move.
10:	Money, the driving force of a journey. Greed.
Jack:	A selfish person.
Queen:	A flirtatious woman.
King:	A rival, a dangerous competitor.

a sneezing fit
his house of cards
collapses

CLUBS:

Ace:	Indicates wealth & fame.
2:	Bad luck. Opposition. Be your own prophet.
3:	New marriage after a friendly divorce.
4:	A dangerous card, showing misfortune.
5:	A marriage or alliance card.
6:	A partnership card. Success by mutual goals.
7:	A card of good luck.
8:	A sense of desperation, urgent need for money.
9:	Represents arguments with good friends.
10:	A card of happiness and good fortune.
Jack:	Represents a good friend, feel better.
Queen:	Represents a long term relationship for a man.
King:	Represents a lifelong companion.

the madame
leads with a high card
no more beer

WARNING:

Every card will give you a playful message in a short letter with playful reflections. Haibun to please you.
Jokerman

ACE OF HEARTS:
Key words: love – romantic – welcoming – fortunate.

Dear Ace of Hearts,
you are sensitive, with a powerful mind in the company of kindred spirits. Sometimes you act suspicious and capricious. Being too trusting causes inconvenience and fumbling. Look out to prevent any misunderstanding and disappointment. Repentance and the silence of a monastery are able to spoil you in hard times. I tell you, don't hesitate, even when a proposal of marriage is in the air. Abandon shyness, you are in bloom, stronger than thought. Sun and moon are your friends. A swallow skims the water.

garden stillness
calming companions
the moon and a cat

I break bread and uncork a good wine. Be my guest. Don't cheat yourself a day longer, change your mind. I am old and ugly enough (as my mum said) to tell you: no need to be cramped for space. Follow your own trails to move in this world. You are not a puppet on a string. Follow your inner path in meditation, the part of you that is true and honest will emerge. Coherence with others and warm affection are hidden treasures, cherish them daily. I play the piano for you.

a knock on the door
his heart beats faster
room service

Jokerman

TWO OF HEARTS:
Key words: beloved – friendly – social – sensitive.

Dear Two of Hearts,
you are neither Rambo nor Catwoman, but simply a beloved lady friend. A jovial, sociable and cheerful person, the clown among small gatherings. No one can beat you in combined action with others. Tiger, what you believe will you receive, until melancholy turns up. It's not awful, observe yourself and feel your remarkable sense for humour. You are not dying yet, unexpected possibilities and spirited chances still exist. What are you waiting for to explore what is really in your mind? Focus on enlightenment.

> *writing haiku*
> *bees as proofreaders*
> *sitting in the sun*

This can be concluded directly: hunting shallowness and frivolities is not your style. You know better. Why should you spoil your life by fear and doubt? Insipidness is not your cup of tea, on the contrary, happiness holds you back. Don't be gloomy, feel the light. Nothing get lost, during the diurnal rotation of the earth. Tai-chi is good for you, the wind rolls the lotus leaves and sweeps the plum blossoms. Step up to seven stars. Suppleness and rootedness are your elements.

> *no body*
> *and no mind*
> *dental floss*

Jokerman

THREE OF HEARTS:
Key words: sensual – creative – affable – tenacious.

Dear Three of Hearts,
mentally you are programmed to win. Sometimes laziness overcomes the workhorse in you, because of this you run into difficulties. You can only find your niche when there's plenty of liquid refreshment? Cheers... however a rebellious liver is pretty awkward. Drinking to excess, by self-pity, always causes complaints about ailments. Make a virtue of necessity, because a pale look and lurid purple eyelids will keep you for a while between the sheets.

> on the table
> the elderberry tea
> sniff that scent

There you go again, tenacious as a pit-bull, to acquire big money and a social status. Of course, what's lacking is a review of your state of affairs or any screening. Never mind, you are flying now and landing is for tomorrow, unless you am making a belly landing by panic or strangling doubts. There is still the certitude of another life, with the glow of paper-lanterns and an attractive gathering.

> on his laptop
> a reading about stress
> he plays patience

Jokerman

FOUR OF HEARTS:
Key words: honest – warm – idealistic – committed.

Dear Four of Hearts,
you are born to serve, what not means that you are a clasp knife or a slave. Universal love, in the broadest sense of the word, is your motive. Compassion for all beings! My friend, take comfort from the ideas of independent minds. Look out for beatific adoration and idolatry. A fanatical admiration has the same baleful influence as racism and bigotry. Chaos is a waste of time, worse than not flossing. We both don't know what the future has in store next. Maybe you will be soon on stage in front of the footlights, to perform the role of your life.

> the snowman
> on his wrinkled hat
> a bread crumb

Don't overshoot yourself with big-headedness, as a peacock is in his pride. King braggart? Sometimes you are fed up with the pressure of work, even before it begins to take shape. I admire your helpful nature and your good power of discernment. You are forbearing with a warm judgement. Brother's keeper, take the plunge! Contact with incense, singing bowls, candlelight or essential oils can strengthen you. Have no doubts, the Bodhi is not the tree!

> *on the pillars*
> *the pomegranates*
> *earth and sky*

Jokerman

FIVE OF HEARTS:
Key words: discreet – bona fide – loving – firm.

Dear Five of Hearts,
you told me that you are a knight, without fear, in the service of widows and orphans? My beloved ones are also my life, that's why I am singing with Jacques Brel: 'Quand on n'a que l'amour.' Love is our pursuit and as well our source of concern. Are you alive and kicking? In full possession of your mental faculties, believing in what you are doing? It's in your nature! The sun emerges in the mountains, fresh dew has not yet dried.

the wild geese
are passing over
stillness arises

There is an adventurous traveler in your blood. You hold on to the helm, as swift as an arrow, after every nasty blow. Tears and heartache are of short duration, unless a wretched job shrivels you up in petulance. Don't let the doom-mongering grumbler awake. Beat the swords into plowshares, until dissatisfaction with your circle of acquaintances turns to malicious wilfulness. I seek out for good company, boisterous people overload our mind. Please, follow your inspiration and conquer the obstacles. React! The plum blossoms open their flowers.

the tomcat
simply arches his back
the dog whines

Jokerman

SIX OF HEARTS:
Key words: wise – adult – phlegmatic – liberal.

Dear Six of Hearts,
since my childhood, I don't avoid experiments, but I stay very carefull so that emotional shocks fail to occur. You make haste slowly, in a flowing style. Conceitedness is not your trademark, you are a man of rank. Not a homebody nor a 'petit bourgeois' dreaming of his own charming little house. No, you are wise, sometimes shy but you don't give up. Typical for a pure go-getter, that's the way it is. I love your self-discipline in 'meditation to think nothing', your self-reflection in the evenings or at the break of day.

> *in the way*
> *of made-up your mind*
> *reading haiku*

Reading is a sacred habit and music put us in motion, but being a backpacker is a different kettle of fish. You drag along personal belongings with you to embellish your hotel room to build yourself a nest. You have a wondrously life, as if by magic, every day is preparing a new adventure. Every contact is blessed with deep meanings. If you discover, with a great sense of romance, a new star in your heart, you invite everyone for a journey to a spiritual centre, a massage parlour, or a swimming pool. I love your green tea. Gyokuru tea, to remember that the greatest human happiness is to bring happiness to many.

> *weltering summer*
> *your shadow plunges already*
> *in the water*

Jokerman

34

SEVEN OF HEARTS:
Key words: human – sensitive – devoted – contemplated.

 7

Hi Seven of Hearts,
are you convinced that love can solve conclusively all problems?
The future of your faithfulness is something at risk, but you know
how to make it. By frivolity? I don't think so. You don't belong to the
breed of seafarers and pioneers, in every harbour a titillating girl.
No 'empire of senses' for you. No squabbling or scorched
emotions. I'm hanged if I know if you have to sprinkle your life with
champagne, but I love looking across your orchards while peace
descends over me. Give me a nip and I sing for you, fine-tuning my
words.

perfume of rum
after to much rum
no more punch

Contrary to a wild youth, you can be a standard bearer for a well-
defined aim: love is the path. You work towards a common goal, in
art and great learning. A well-considered judgement, good
experiences and crystal-clear insights hasten to help. Hear all, see
all, say nothing? New inspiration and stringent agreements w˙ it for
you, if all your activities are geared to a life in beauty. One-way
traffic is strictly taboo.

in my rice bowl
only a fortune cookie
do not touch

Jokerman

EIGHT OF HEARTS:
Key words: tolerant – understanding – quiet – inspiring.

Eight of Hearts,
dear eager beaver and whiz-kid with a functional brain. Duty writes itself in capitals, even for you, usually simmering until the deadline appears on the calendar. On that moment, you come rushing, frenetically, to manage the job. You mind what you are doing, bribery is lurking everywhere. You've got to be clever: he that mischief hatches, mischief catches! I love to read your poetry describing sacred places and meditation as vital forces for creative thinking. You inspire me to ask: 'When your dream is no longer a dream, what will you do?'

> *the frog*
> *sits like you and me*
> *making faces*

All in all, you have more good prospects with a bright and breezy character, if capriciousness don't knocks you down. Keep your appointments, be your own prophet! Gnoothi se auton! Your future beams and brings emotions to the surface. You make progress, enjoy a high income. The silence in your inner temple is venerable as freshly baked bread. You gain inspiration for fairy tales, alert enough for new contacts and appointments. I love the Buddha in my friends.

> *the thin outline*
> *of the crescent moon*
> *in your sunglasses*

Jokerman

NINE OF HEARTS:
Key words: optimistic – charitable – conscious – positive.

 9

Dear Nine of Hearts,
the common good and solidarity are your key words. Besides love and affection, there is your eye for business discussions and transactions, even if a safe in Suisse is not your intended purpose. Private ownership is not your first vocation. You prefer descending the depths of feelings for their full value. You have a preference for ethical behaviour, greed is not your aim. Your explicit temperament can be silly: saying the daftest things, being in no time with your head in the clouds or kissing the earth with a hell of a smack.

seaweedy
and pronounced
your bourbon

Spiritual growth and joy of life have a meeting point in your contemplative mind. Wisdom appeals in sacrifices. I adore shells and corals, you like desert sand and gurgling mountain streams. Making new discoveries, comparing events and integration are perfect possibilities to demonstrate the authenticity of your being. To make connections is your real aim. Even for you, one day Zen becomes Zen.

a shakuhachi
between the peach trees
nothing to say

Jokerman

TEN OF HEARTS:
Key words: compassion – harmony – peace – independence.

 10

Dear Ten of Hearts,
the outside world can blow warm and cold, you face the future undismayed. I drink to the prosperity of your undertakings, you are a lucky dog. The Devil's own luck is your part, slices of good fortune are present. Art with a capital 'A' makes you happy. You find rest for your mind and body in relationship between the events and close connections with others. Refine what it means to be human with your commitment.

> *tsunami*
> *a tourist crying*
> *for her jewels*

You believe in heart and brains, feel with your brain and think with your heart. You are neither a cracking jumping jack nor a short firework, rather a smouldering and glowing fire. Always an incorrigible optimist, you move between pure harmony and eternal bickering. Burning love? You play a defensive game. Your house (of cards) is still hospitable, you open your doors to strangers and acquaintances alike. Do I dare to cuddle you? You are aware, loving the glorification of beauty with an independent mind. You are not afraid of anxious days and solitude. Do you know the sound of one hand clapping? Silence!

> *color and wind*
> *unite in the Grand Canyon*
> *tinkling raindrops*

Jokerman

JACK OF HEARTS:
Key words: hearty – guiltless – enjoyment – charity.

 J

Dear Jack of Hearts,
why do I want to save this world so urgently? You take everyone under your protection: grandpa, grandma, your thirteen little brothers and sisters, my two Siamese tomcats and a naked poodle. Pure charity? That's to me to discover. You skedaddle if I reject your unsolicited assistance. Please travel over the world as a slightly eccentric womanizer. Haul away the terrible suffering of the whole nasty and iniquitous world. It's no fun drinking water, I prefere a good old Balvenie. Let's have a toast my buddy.

sitting on a swing
after a drinking spree
splitting headache

Are you an inveterate self-seeker, a nonchalant romantic or a hot lady-killer? Once in a while the faithful lover and the a wily fellow are blended. As a merrymaker you know how to enjoy life, with honeyed words. Sugar Daddy! You appear happily frolicking as a flamboyant birthday boy especially on your delightful parties, without buggering about pranks and tricks. Gathering knowledge is your second nature. Needless to say that I believe in your intelligence and also in a great sense of romance by moonlight. Have a candlelit dinner in Paris, Milan... The champagne spirit of celebration is with you.

a mosquito
flies trough the night
star gazing

Jokerman

QUEEN OF HEARTS:
Key words: charming – amiable – expressive – hospitality.

Dear Queen of Hearts,
I move in on of the best circles, charmed by your inviting feelings. As a good wizard, I love art for art's sake! Your metaphorical language and fairy tales belong to my world in witch elves, gnomes and unicorns have a wonderful niche. Pookahs and goblins can gain sometimes the upper hand, but my attention don't vanish, because I don't reveal you as a greedy temptress. You are not balancing on the very edge of voluptuous frivolity. No sex with Madonna!

on trial
behind your hand fan
a jeering laugh

I love an innocent flirtation! More, I am capable of being a sexy lover. So lend me a helping hand and I will always be there if you help me discover magic and challenges: rituals, temples, gem stones, incense, haiku books or kung-fu. You feel that the earth is your body, your teacher? Earth is my portal to imagination. You do your guests well on a set table, in an excellent atmosphere. I taste you wine, with pleasure. Yes, I am your dreamy-eyed friend. I meditate about your pebbles in the river. A white snake sticks out its tongue.

with solemn peace
as proud as a peacock
a peacock

Jokerman

KING OF HEARTS:
Key words: paternal – quiet – peaceful – mild.

Dear King of Hearts,
I lie in my hammock, dreaming of an elves night on the island Man. The cooler close at hand: white wine with a few balm leaves. A toast to an amiable man with fatherly tenderness. You are a spiritual director and a good guide. You like to meditate with oneness of your mind. Your everyday life renewed, sharing personal happiness with many others.

dreaming of her
a Playboy magazine
under your pillow

Boozing it up at a beanfeast with a lot of hubbub is not your aim. Sensitivity first, because sometimes you are grumpy like an old skinflint. It'll probably get better in time. more focused on inner peace and seasonal beauty. Enlightenment and amazement will come with the true joy of life and with more concentration on your everyday routine. I am grateful for the quince and the roses in your garden. Were you reading Hildegard of Bingen, the twelfth-century Rhineland visionary? I am singing Beatle-songs. We both enjoy fireworks and talking with our ancestors. I feel inner silence in every fibre of your being. You love informal talks on Zen meditation.

raising the sail
with the moonrise
above the waves

Jokerman

ACE OF SPADES:
Key words: energetic – clever – wise – powerful.

Dear Ace of Spades,
variations on one theme: you have a warm preference for reason. Input: 'Je pense donc je suis.' You are eager to learn. Occasionally, the price is alienation. Luckily your heart is full of passion. Everything fascinates you if there is enough mystery. Don't talk rubbish, with consideration and communication we will realize miracles.

> *you shovel snow*
> *in your tappit-hen*
> *a hot whisky*

Coping with all your feelings is a labour of Hercules. Perseverance will bring understanding and wisdom. The dissenting view of your friends gains a clearer understanding. It is but a step from the sublime to the ridiculous. Patience is a fine thing. The sea is unmoved while the waves move. I hear the wind, he journeys trough the forests. You are whispering that the oaks and the copper beeches are our brothers. Rainy nights tell us about little sparrows, floating clouds and the turn of the year. Let's talk more, there is a path of enlightenment for everyone.

> *your first dream*
> *of the New Year*
> *a labyrinth*

Jokerman

TWO OF SPADES:
Key words: serene – controversial – philosophical – silent.

Dear Two of Spades,
they characterize you with pet names as: mule, stubborn, troublemaker, awkward so-and-so and other charming names. You accept these teasing blows. Indeed, there is no perfect man and in a way the pretension of humankind is empty. Harmony needs self-knowledge. A change of air will do us good. Trains, boats and planes. Visiting the temples of Katmandu, parade 'les boulevards de Paris', the beach and the Japanese garden in Ostend. Be my guest.

the scent
of fresh buckwheat
opens memories

You prefer to read in silence, to memorize the planets, the wild pinks in flower and the old sea slug boats of Zanzibar, learning as a withdrawn student with a beginners mind. Life is a great book full of secrets. Its amazing; you absolutely love it. Memories are vivacious. Smell the ripe mangos of Patan, the incense of Istanbul, the wine of Burgundy, the unleavened bread of the Bedouin in the Sinai-desert. Let's taste fresh water, sweet-smelling fruits and young vegetables. Drop by for a good conversation, let's discuss it over a glass of wine.

in my garden
a crooked cucumber
good day sunshine

Jokerman

THREE OF SPADES:
Key words: stabel – hopeful – tolerant – cautious.

 3

Dear Three of Spades,
chaos and sadness can be part of our life. I accept to learn, knowing when to speak is often less of an art than knowing when not to. You are stable and forbearing enough. You stand firm, but do I easily admit my blunders? Do we act with great caution? It comes as no surprise, shilly-shallying exists. No problem, nothing gets lost. So please let me hear, in the stillness of your stone garden, your end-blown Japanese bamboo flute, playing 'A Bell Ringing in the Empty Sky', a piece which the monk Kyochiku Zenshi received in a dream while asleep in Koku Zodo Temple. We are members of the universe, parts of the world.

a shakuhachi
ripples in the pond
by a few koi

Humour is our salvation. The playful man is on the way. I know, changing is a matter of course, most certainly if self-confidence took a severe blow. Terrible ordeals and financial matters are often banks of the same river. Watch out with melancholy. Hear the silence, nothing can be lost.

painted on
a Japanese folding fan
another fan

Jokerman

FOUR OF SPADES:
Key words: charitable – emotional – sensitive – skilled.

Dear Four of Spades,
your bookcase is large. You always have your nose in a book: Matsuo Bashō, Lee Gurga, Jane Reichhold, Jack Kerouac, William J. Higginson, Michael Moore and many other tomes. Close encounters of the first kind. Brother, nobody will notice doubts about your ready knowledge. Yes, once in a while you have two left hands, but to be clumsy is no disgrace if you are playful and a charitable judge of human characters. Welcome firewater and bonbonnière!

nosing and tasting
you smell sweetness
on the malting floor

Are you upset because you are upset? Beautiful paradox. Listen to an old song: the open country will bring rest for your mind and body. Brooding about an idea? Always look on the bright side of life, many creative ideas are waiting in the shelter of your meditation about 'do not kill'. Let your Himalayan singing bowls reverberate. Beat the big drum and burn sweet incense.

the monk bows
for the mango tree
a bowl sings

Jokerman

FIVE OF SPADES:
Key words: playful – creative – linguistic – humorous.

Dear Five of Spades,
do you know yourself? Sorry, once in a while I can be so whimsical and capricious. Under the influence I even dare to piss a haiku in the snow. Triviality? Revise our plans, delay and reconsideration are the results. No problem, I'll quit the job if necessary. Don't cry for me. Dream on. I am giving your baby his first bath, I read you an inspiring story about a Buddhist deity and I play marbles. Do you bake pancakes?

> *your perfume*
> *of fruity and ripe raisin*
> *kiss me again*

I am firm on this issue of love: I will easily recommence. By steadfastness of character and a pinch of badgering. As a Gemini you have to follow your own track, even on a narrow road to Oku. Idem dito for a married life, with divorce(s) as result. Your mood changes and varies somewhat? Indeed, but you don't laze around on your ass. The quicksilver in your blood is so active. Welcome the changes. Let's spy out the land, in an exploration of the metropolis, the souks and the graveyards. Tell me the story behind the scenery of Arches. I saw the 'Three Gossips' and 'Balanced Rock', frozen in time.

> *Ryokan seems foolish*
> *but the road is very wide*
> *you take a plane*

JOKERMAN

SIX OF SPADES:
Key words: intuitive – tender – sensitive – meditative.

Dear Six of Spades,
your intuition is phenomenal! A must for a discerning man of extremes. I adopt in my life a middle course, you strike a happy medium. Our life offers a lot of opportunities: diligence besides deftness, great precision besides the patience of a saint. Bear in mind, the changeable and cyclic movements. It will protect us against a good deal of troubles. Allow yourself to be delighted with the daily beauty and challenges: seeking, harmless speaking, dreaming and dancing the dances of innocent jokers. I perform a crazy puppet show for you.

a young mother
sings a cradlesong
fanning her baby

Contact with wise men or guiltless fools? Powerful masters and nutty bunglers, notice they have the same breathing. A nimbleness mind prevents that you kick up a rumpus. I prefer to talk about opportunity scouting, not about problem solving. Imagine: (s)tones, crawfishes, cabbage white butterflies, flowerpots, maybeetles. In fact everything on earth reveals to us the pure emotion of our sensory perception.

after midnight
the crunching of chains
a cat on the swing

Jokerman

47

SEVEN OF SPADES:
Key words: punctual – independent – humanitarian – go-getter.

Dear Seven of Spades,
let there be light in your inner temple. The feared roof tile will not cleave your scull, the stepladder will not break down and your canoe will not sink like a stone. Have no fear. Doom-mongering is needless. You are well balanced if you avoid speculation. A contemplative mind is your best friend on your winding road. What you see is you, a Grand Sheik, a gypsy dancer and a damn good storyteller. Someday, we will discover that all problems are illusions. Ring the bells.

> *after the polka*
> *from the barrel organ*
> *the sound of coins*

A dream seems to be a royal road to our subconscious. All the cultures on Earth have attached, at all times, significance to the dream world. Life gives our story a twist. Follow your inner guide, whatever (s)he can be. Amazing possibilities are waiting, wake them up. You are everywhere, touring the world and dreaming in guesthouses, gathering forces as it comes around. Your sweet song has the feel of a cycle that can go on forever. Don't shoot the pianist, he is Thelonious Monk!

> *one blue note*
> *a haiku on itself*
> *the jazz concert*

Jokerman

EIGHT OF SPADES:
Key words: strong-willed – energetic – pleasing – fast.

Dear Eight of Spades,
my road runs straight on to the high towering mountains. Don't worry about me, I believe in a new world full of kindness and deep compassion. Needless to make a racket, don't be so noisy. I am not confused or kinky by my or your duality. I can be an honorary member of a club or lead a retired life between my pear trees, Abyssinian cats and prayer wheels. I listen to your gong-strokes and whistling.

effortless
your warm jazz riffs
and nutty haiku

Heartfelt contact is the aim. I avoid thoughtless behaviour, guide me gently to the countryside, tell me about invoking the ancestors and special meals. Be my witness when I walk back home or fly to foreign countries. I pay my respects to your cathedrals and megalithic tombs. Let me hear your stories about the spinning dervishes. I make a pilgrimage to your garden. Pour out your famous green tea as liquid amber. Old Taoist, let me observe the beauty of the dawn. Bird shadows sink in distant mist, bell tone emerge. I hear your noble chanting.

a bright moon
its reflection appears
in her cup of tea

Jokerman

NINE OF SPADES:
Key words: helpful – playful – passionate – instinctive.

Dear Nine of Spades,
you are wide awake! A sense of humour is created, not born. Playfulness as company name is just a front, you don't bother about my future, you see the stillness in everything's moving. Indeed, I move easily in the world. Our love is understood as the meeting of two independent rascals. We have many points of agreement: our bantering is a wonderful game and we love both to crack bawdy jokes. Sorry honourable and high-born ladies, but it will happen again. For a thousand ages we share this style. What evening is our evening in France?

> *on chante*
> *et on joue l'accordéon*
> *les vignerons*

Hopefully, the frog will change into a Prince in the coming days. Today I am a still a harum-scarum, a beachcomber talking with shifting sands and starfishes. I see the sea before cockcrow. Show me shells and mermaids in broad daylight. If conditions are favourable I welcome a change: new friends, new companionship. You ask me to dance? Tell me the story of our origins and the sad shadows of our past: Auschwitz, Hiroshima, May Lai, Falusha! Beat, tap and caress your single-stringed berimbeau. Sing me a childlike tune. Only the clouds are moving...

> *merrymakers*
> *so bloody noisy*
> *for his hung*

Jokerman

TEN OF SPADES:

Key words: brave – happiness – cleverness – humour.

 10

Dear Ten of Spades,
you are a fluent speaker with a good sense of humour. Self-teaching shouldn't cause you any surprise, only a lack of self-confidence is alarming. I don't deny your intuition, I hear your voice of happiness which stands the test of everyday life. Sure, you can talk the hind leg off a donkey. To cover up your feelings? Alright, sit down and play me a languorous Paul McCartney song to cherish our inner peace.

plunging a bottle
champagne into ice
Valentine's Day

New life, it doesn't come easy if we are rooted in habits. I put my other concerns aside for a moment, I won't miss your first appearance on the pulpit. Just pretend I am not there. Talk without cackling. Never stop peddling your theories about profound experiences in the wild desert. Offer me an amusing glimpse of your cleverness, talking about baby scorpions, colorless but free. Keep away from boisterous tomfoolery. Empty yourself and return to your source: stillness. Take a walk on the seaside, create deeper attention to see how fortunate we all are.

along the beach
under the sun tan lotion
a lot of silicone

Jokerman

51

JACK OF SPADES:
Key words: idealistic – supple – smart – nonconformist.

Dear Jack of Spades,
you, the captain is speaking: 'Welcome on board!'
I know that you raise your eyebrows inquiringly when I talk about
adulthood and our ability to put things in perspective. Your
searching mind brings you everywhere, as a crepuscular
photographer active in the cooler hours of dusk, as a chess-player
in a teagarden, as a comforter for hermits in a melancholy mood.
Use your brains, and avoid having debts. Look into the mirror of the
32 points on the compass, meet kite and kittens, chalices and
spinning wheels. Explore a drowned valley, feel petrified wood and
sit in silent enjoyment. The sunset illumines the villages.

> *a caterpillar*
> *in undulating motion*
> *dreaming of the sky*

One should not discuss a dream about playing cards? It is said: 'if
you see yourself in your dreams playing cards, then you will soon
fall in love.' Please don't ring the author. Don't believe to much in
the interpretations of your dreams, or you will run up against
difficulties. The ultimate proof is in the eating: if you believe me.
you are in troubles!

> *snowman*
> *even the ice*
> *is lent to us*

Jokerman

QUEEN OF SPADES:
Key words: logical – elegance – observing – fair.

 Q

Dear Queen of Spades,
you say that a haiku-workshop strikes you as being an old boys club. You have the idea that a haiku-circle is rather a club where the old fart sits atop his self-made mountain while the others cheer him on. Do you mean he pontificates while others imitate him? Do they have a good time doing it, slapping each other's backs, saying what a good job they all did? No my dear, a lot of poets are inspired, writing with an impassioned language, discussing discoveries in life, love and caresses.

> *reading Shiki*
> *dangling roses*
> *around you*

We all have an urgent need for tenderness, without obvious excuses. My naked bride, rice-paper panels and a piano are lining this room, let me be your urban fisherman, your passionate lover. We can make love on the sisal matting, daydreaming about writing or reading senryū. Sweetness on our tongues. I am a pilgrim from a far-off country, feeling an intimate companionship with all seasons and nature in all its tenderness.

> *little buddha*
> *on the lacquered table*
> *I touch her nipples*

Jokerman

KING OF SPADES:
Key words: active – honourable – devoted – tender.

Dear King of Spades,
I adore your warm tuned judgement and commitment. Stone, sisal and polished wood are the materials that define your music room. I sing a song for you, whispering in your ear about your beauty, caressing flowers, seeking answers for my confusion. Remember my footprints on your banks, see my fragrant plants crowded on the rooftop. Look at our garden between the clouds.

> gazing with wonder
> a butterfly on your hair
> hold a mirror

A warm sound sings in soundscapes and your improvisations. You are surrounded by several bronze coloured bowls. Hear a wide range of soft percussion. I knock the rim of a twelve-inch singing bowl with a crooked wand. Several overtones pulsate brightly in enveloping your body. This sound-experience is new for you, as if the tones come out of your soul to stabilize your feelings and emotions. Go beyond earth's lamentations and self-pity. Enjoy good health.

> sitting in front
> of a snow-covered buddha
> a bowl on your palm

Jokerman

ACE OF DIAMONDS:
Key words: creative – constructive – diligent – freedom.

 1

Dear Ace of Diamonds,
you are balancing between the money-grubbers and the testimony of Zen master Poe-tai Ho-Shang. I listen to the music of the man from Utopia, Frank Zappa. So dance with me for peace the Sheik Yerbouti tango, dance with a Jewish princess or a Palestinian beauty. An illusion is both real and unreal, as it is perceived through your eyes. The nature of my dreams and your memory is the same. The pack of foxes is pleased, the mountain woods are quiet; trouts know the depth of the cold streams.

> *stormy wind*
> *dreaming of twisters*
> *blossoms at dawn*

My so called 'iron-clad certainty' has much to do with a touch of irony and even self-mockery. After all who cares? Haiku are connected with 'all and sundry' if you like so. Freedom of choice! The 'do's and don'ts' are not my cup of tea, I am too young for such interminable discussions. But I always ask the haiku-scene in question, without self-invented 'mastership' nor complacency. Learning is asking. Right or wrong... I try to write haiku... floating free. Haiku and haibun are not *from* the heart, they are written *with* a heart. On this point I am my own prophet and I enjoy reading & writing. Do you?

> *crunching snow*
> *and grandfather's clogs*
> *writing memories*

Jokerman

TWO OF DIAMONDS:
Key words: involved – aware – helpful – persistent.

 2

Dear Two of Diamonds,
travel without fear, move up and down between glaring contrasts and contradictions. Move between the mud huts from Tanzania and the desert tents from Tunisia. Move between woodlands and snowy canyons. The world is yours. Have the power to transform your anger into enlightenment. You and I are united in painful loss with bated breath, in sweet dreams and expectations. The drinks go down easy, another little French brandy will take the strain.

> *after gulping down*
> *so many drinks*
> *a lift failure*

I burst into a roar of laughter, your wall is a fool's paper. Your graffiti have pretty colours. Thanks for your funny stories about pure gain and painful tattoos. Don't put on a mask, let's poke fun at the lady next door. Tell her about the thousand cats you saw in Istanbul, tell her about the horses in Mongolia, sing your love songs. Deep inside your bar-talk, I can feel that there are plenty of storms on every ocean. Hear Chris Rea on slide guitar, dancing down the stony road.

> *the lady next door*
> *naked at the bus stop -*
> *Alzheimer's*

Jokerman

THREE OF DIAMONDS:
Key words: courage – messenger – positive – enterprising.

 3

Old friend Three of Diamonds,

you still undress the waitress from Chili with your eyes, randy as an old goat. The snow was falling when I met you for the first time, some years back. Both on shaky legs and a faraway look. Yes, extremes meet, you a lucky-son-of-a-bitch and I am just me. The big world is a small sheep house. I don't pretend to understand your messages but I love your puns on obscene words and your original mind inspired by silly whims.

he gorges himself
with salted chips
loneliness

A right-angled tear in the green baize, smoke-stained. You, old heart and guiltless skirt-chaser, you need contemplation for a while. Your mind is a playful puzzle, your forehead furrowed. I think that the past is staring you in the face, tickling your heart and offering peace of mind. Relax your fingers and fasten your banjo, sing that you were born in Portland Town.

to much sake
he grabs his chopsticks
unsteady

Jokerman

FOUR OF DIAMONDS:
Key words: realistic – prosperous – influential – dogged.

Dear Four of Diamonds,
you admire the smart and hilarious books written by Michael Moore, lampooning the greed, arrogance and corruption of unscrupulous people. What with the 'ownership society' and her fictitious reasons to start a war, beltway politics, revenge and manipulation? You listen to the stories of people, even if they are very sad. For example about 9/11 in the country of George of Arabia. Let the kids start praying.

> *in the picture*
> *covered with stars and stripes*
> *thousand body bags*

I still love your beloved country. Certainly if it cares about 'our' world, without sinking in self-centered despair and cynicism. I visited once the Grand Canyon. I was greatly touched, with a squirrel on my hand, in the impressive stone cathedral of Bryce. I saw rock art symbols, drawings of power lines and Kachina masks in Petrified Forest. Deer dancers? I played a few singing bowls on crimson red rocks for world peace. Encouraged by a wise Navajo Indian. May his spirit walk in beauty!

> *gathering wood*
> *the whoosh*
> *of eagle wings*

Jokerman

FIVE OF DIAMONDS:
Key words: harmonious – hot – research – spiritual.

My learned friend Five of Diamonds,
your free and improvised music has a natural sound. I find myself
dazzled during your piano solo with tremendous tremolo and
exquisite pedaling. In concert with explorations of contemporary
music. Vibrating in clusters of sounds, one note vibrates. The
whole pub is humming. I close my eyes, lecturing in my memory. I
am at the same time on various locations, different as chalk and
cheese. I am flying a Piper above the Golden River of my town, I
am a visitor in the St. Catherine's Monastery on Mount Sinai, I am
standing at Ground Zero. The humming is inside me, tears in my
eyes.

> *in the garden*
> *a humming bumblebee*
> *reading your letter*

Notes of power. I am walking on the beach after your very poignant
concert. Thinking of all the details of changing in your music, with
clusters for daylight and blue notes for times gone by. Is your inner
ear developed? I hear the waves, hear the sounds. Feel the notes.
Be power of silence my friend, I would like to explore more of your
poetical music. Jan Garbarek, one day in March I go down to the
sea and listen.

> *on the piano stool*
> *in admiration for Chopin*
> *a calico cat*

Jokerman

SIX OF DIAMONDS:
Key words: strong – noble – generous – headstrong.

Dear Six of Diamonds,
you can talk till your blue in the face, improving our good understanding. We chatter about hermits and pilgrims, books of photographs. A bit peculiar 'savoir vivre' in late evenings of talk. The sun is halfway up, we scarcely touch our Galardón 'premium' tequila, we discuss for ours blue agaves and unexpected windfalls. I am quietly confident, new challenges will cross your path.

> *fragrant smoke*
> *of roasted chestnuts*
> *Brussels by night*

How did you get here, going astray between stretches of green and old weather-beaten walls? Tell me the secret story of these historic parts of town. What about the old pubs and the common alehouses with smoke-filled curtains? I see a brothel-keeper in dim red light, a bashful dog with a timorous look and your sagging knees. Dear friend, show me the way to the next apron, touch me with languorous notes in soft spotlight. Play you double bass old buddy so that we can reach the stars.

> *double bass*
> *and soft toe-tapping*
> *basically taps*

Jokerman

SEVEN OF DIAMONDS:
Key words: love – enthusiasm – joyful – mature.

Dear Seven of Diamonds,
I hear your question: prosperity or well-being? After some hesitation you opted for the latter. Boredom is not your aim. You can fly high without poppycock and trifles. You want no cheap amusement, no horseplay for you. Even if you are rolling in money. You avoid being flat broke, you go very carefully and act with great caution in fair trade, attaining happiness within the flow of days.

in your mailbox
between the birthday cards
a tax form

May I say that you are mature? You visited many exotic places on our planet, saw pintados and pink deserts. You may not think of yourself as a spiritual giant, but you don't need to be a master to be a soul brother for someone else. That's the way you act, sometimes as a clown, but mostly as a light-hearted friend wearing rose-colored glasses. I think you are a fine reminder to develop an attitude of gratitude. In a flash, once in a while, you are singing old songs about koans and against greed, the sword that kills mankind.

strike the gong
for world peace
a long echo

Jokerman

EIGHT OF DIAMONDS:
Key words: successful – leadership – balanced – firm.

 8

Dear Eight of Diamonds,
greed is your enemy! There's no need to rush things, ripe apples fall without saying. You enjoy talking with merchants and fishermen as well as with your friends. You dare to ask foolish questions, laughing and joking. You get a great deal of pleasure, listening to amusing stories with a note of irony. You are irresistibly amiable, dancing defiantly with the village people.

> *my pretty darling*
> *during your belly dance*
> *I come too soon*

Sitting on a bench in your garden, I adore breathing in the perfume of rosemary and thyme, while you are playing the old accordion so skilfully, performing a mysterious dance. One should not discuss the harmonies of your music. I stay tuned and listen. I do not speak because my words cannot describe the colour of your notes. The ultimate beauty is not even to think.

> in the grass
> the prints off bike tires
> his music corner

Jokerman

NINE OF DIAMONDS:
Key words: independent – character – individual – straight.

Dear Nine of Diamonds,
you are a hardcore kid, dreaming of ultimate freedom, not directly in search to feel divine light. You told me that there is no ego and no self! Maybe you mean that there is only total awakening, and even no Buddha. Is our world an illusion? You kick against the chaos in our modern society, you are vegan running for animal rights.

> a dog is dying
> needles in his brain
> for her cosmetics

There's dissatisfaction and a sudden lurch, you act forcefully as the singer-songwriter of your band. No, I can not trade you for a sweet-voiced nightingale but I've got your messages: stop the killing, meat is murder. This litany sounds familiar to me, review as objectively as you can, the evidence of this matter. Can we wake up and change our mind? Or is this only romantic talk? Indeed, I agree everything is connected and alive. As above, so below!

> on his arm
> tattooed in black
> Snow White

Jokerman
dedicated to my son Jonas

TEN OF DIAMONDS:
Key words: rich – social – solid – smart.

Dear Ten of Diamonds,
was it getting on your nerves too, all that nagging about spiritual rules, unwritten or not? Do me a favour! Charlatans and tricksters can go to hell for all I care. Do we really need endless claptrap about gateless gates, fire-walking and other money-grubbery? Can a real heart's message be delivered in small talk? Restfulness is not for sale, inner peace is for free. Collecting preaching material is easy but can the care of souls be done by bank account?

> *facing Daruma*
> *the first Zen patriarch*
> *he blows bubbles*

To err seems to be human, let's go for a walk and think twice. I follow you on the small tracks, you gather blackberries. Delicious. A roof of dense foliage disguises the sunbeams, shadows play leapfrog in the verges. We sit down for a few charcoal sketches. The wind whispers sweet nothings. I think he knows that the essence of our mind is not born yet. The silence is endless.

> *in a sketch*
> *the persistent rain*
> *sssssssstillness*

Jokerman

JACK OF DIAMONDS:
Key words: competent – ingenious – valuable – creative.

 J

Dear Jack of Diamonds,
beat attentive your feathered drum, while you invoke the spirits of
water and fire, air en earth. Offer spicy incense of sandalwood and
aloe into the four wind directions. Sit in lotus position, with an open
mind. Hold on not one splinter of the past. Meet all the forms of the
death in your every day contemplations. You are learning the art of
dying. Be without fear. Honour the death in your life, your life in the
death. Meditate without resistance. Confirm harmony in the
melodies of your shamanic songs. The eternal wheel of the
seasons rotate soundless, around and around.

> *worshippers*
> *gathered in a cave*
> *the drums still*

The wind is romping with a whistling voice between the black
bamboo stems. Observe without judgement. A first autumn leaf
whirls down. Mushrooms grow in clusters. The autumnal wood is
embraced by twisted wisps of mist. The smoke of myrrh spiral up
as a fragrant offering. The dusk is red as the sap of an alder-bask. I
enjoy the melodious sound of your temple bells.

> *hailstones*
> *tinkling on windchimes*
> *a shaman prays*

Jokerman

QUEEN OF DIAMONDS:
Key words: purposeful – animation – vitality – charming.

Darling Queen of Diamonds,
you touch my heart my midnight star, and it happens with passion
my well-beloved Queen. Take me to your studio and show me your
new paintings with blossoming trees, canyoned paths and wild pink
flowers. Be wild.

hunchbacked tree
in tones of black and grey
ink on paper

Duke Ellington plays the piano and I, a simple soul, kiss your
plunging neckline. I fall in love with you, so please dance with me
now to your rooms of imagination. Let's taste fresh olives, goat's
cheese and sparkling wine. Offer me your personal guidance to
your pleasure garden. We, the beauty and the beast, are bursting
with life, both beautiful winners with strong energy and a creative
and powerful mind. Be my wild flower. Touch me, charming
protectress of my heart and I write your gentle name on the new
calendar, while you are asleep. Soften my feelings with poetical
stories about haiku poets, show me your path to the sea. I am your
stray cat. I purr.

dewdrops
on the pomegranates
footpath by dawn

Jokerman

KING OF DIAMONDS:
Key words: organizer – handy – skilful – refinement.

Dear King of Diamonds,
you live between the colossal pine-trees and the purple asters near the waterfalls. Throughout your whole life, you was a nomadic craftsman; on the road between settlements and small hamlets to wear your bowls and bells. Getting on in years, you found serenity in the mountains under the cloudy sky and the endless views. I look at your skilful hands moulding bowls from snow and ice, and I remark that your bowls will never sing. You nod and smile: "Indeed, they will melt to become liquid silence."

snowman
a frozen blackbird
on your hat

We plod along through the snow, stripped to the waist. We rub snow on each other's back, without shiver. The cold opens an invisible door of consciousness for two old fellows seeking inspiration for modest wisdom. We laugh and cry at the same time, happy madcaps with nothing to lose. Love and being well-balanced are one. I love the simplicity of mother earth.

three sparrows
on the frozen bucket
crumb-sweepers

Jokerman

ACE OF CLUBS
Key words: original – versatile – jovial – generous.

 1

Dear Ace of Clubs,
we are sword-fighters in the interval between exercises to discover our own magical sound world. Bowls and bells invite us to invent our own music. What kind of methods are available? Just be a musician! Music is a mirror that shows you your own spiritual, mental and physical forces. No better means than music to unite to people. All the instruments affirm that music is called the 'Divine Art'.

> *new year's letter*
> *grandpa is greatly touched*
> *tickling the ivories*

Be all ears in workshops, factories, shop floors and garages. A circular saw sometimes sings better than a good Javanese gong. Certain anvils, oil barrels and brake drums have a melodious voice. Try to buy yourself some Turkish copper coffee bowls, the sound is amazing. Tunisian mortars also have a unique sound. Music is linked with the origin of life itself, the notes are the primordial vibration of divine energy. See the stars and listen to the harmony of the spheres. Sing, while your guitar gently weeps.

> *your staff notation*
> *the moonlit valley*
> *as composer*

Jokerman

TWO OF CLUBS:
Key words: valiant – confident – inquisitive – harmonizing.

Dear Two of Clubs,
you teach me that haiku writing is a kind of hopping: once in awhile being in the blue sky! Flying on my own wings. Going nuts, without the illusions of my mind. I know that the past of humanity is very childish. Even when I got all the degrees that the art school can offer, I am still ignorant. Scholarship will not teach us, no problem if we open up our eyes to be afire and alive in wisdom, purposeless as a bird on the wing. In fact freedom comes only with wisdom, no university can offer nor create it. Get lost once in a while to find yourself.

> *suspicious*
> *you examine the core*
> *dear blackbird*

See the bird, at ease with himself. As far as your life is concerned you have to live it on your own way. Walk quiet canyons were red rocks glow, share in luminous stormlight the creative forces, yet rarely seen. See along your walk the floodwaters, the rumbling thunderheads and the lightning. Soak your feet in plunge pools, listen how water drips. Hear the flock of bighorn sheep. Close your eyes.

> *a squall line*
> *the dog howls*
> *in snatches*

Jokerman

THREE OF CLUBS:
Key words: self-confident – cool – cheerful – attractive.

 3

Dear Three of Clubs,
you walk on stilts surrounded by fire-eaters and jugglers, armed with a warm vision. In your mind you create your own Cirque du Soleil. Travel with me in your imagination. My goal is to embrace your dream. Dear clown, comment the power of the special light effects in a starry night. Play the first fiddle in a celebration of music. Invite me for a metaphoric journey which starts high in the snowy mountains. We are living in the fast lane, delighted about life.

> acrobatic
> flying trapeze artists
> dad looks away

You are transforming my energy. Dear clown, you try to make things nice and cozy, so take me for a journey through your fantastic and timeless fairy tales. You are singing about hidden mysteries at Chartres cathedral. Telling stories about secret powers of magician-lords, desperate housewifes and their fragile sweethearts, birds of passage and the phoenix rising from the ashes. The black horse of the death and the white horse of solar light gallop in your ballads. Are you a haiku troubadour?

> the clown
> on his tombstone
> a red nose

Jokerman

FOUR OF CLUBS:
Key words: acute – clever – dynamic – steady.

 4

Dear Four of Clubs,

I left my wood sandals at the entrance. I bow for the porcelain Buddha on your Oriental chest. His small statue is standing on your books about hardcore music and the poetry of Allen Ginsberg, piled high. A selection of prints illustrates in a dreamy fashion the 'Fabulous Four' from Liverpool. Outside, one flowering plum blossom against a background of misty clouds. Kung-fu on the beach is waiting for you. The sand will talk.

> *sleeping dunes*
> *can you hear the snow*
> *from across the sea*

Sit down in front of the sea; caress the sand. Breathe peacefully. Throw open your mind for the waves. Let them go through your soul. Keep breathing peacefully. Enjoy the spirit of the sea, take a shell upon your open palm or upon the tips of your fingers. Relax. Thank the sea when there is silence in the big fuss of your mind. Set him free, in remembrance of Naropa's words: 'My mind is the perfect Buddha, my speech is the perfect teaching, my body is the perfect spiritual community.' Open your eyes.

> after midnight
> a bath in the North Sea
> in your birthday suit

Jokerman
dedicated to my son Hans & Barbara

FIVE OF CLUBS:
Key words: adventurous – sensual – open – familiar.

 5

Dear Five of Clubs,
in our childhood, once I had a second-hand piano at home. I was the only one to open up the lid to play a few crunching and creaky notes. I tried to take it naturally with an intuitive feeling, but the frame of the piano was distorted and pulled out of position. Dad wasn't kidding. The piano went to your basement room, there you ruined the piano completely.

> *playing the piano*
> *since you past away*
> *so many blue notes*

Today, I play once again the piano, not with the 'trilling treble' and 'rolling bass' of Martial Solal or Fred van Hove, with their ability to play one hand against the other at a different tempo, and sometimes in different keys. No, I am forced to choose a more modest 'free-flying' and meditative way... luckily with your injection of humour. You play even on the inside of the piano with felt-tipped small beaters because a prepared piano opens a completely new range of unusual and dramatic sounds. Indeed, undreamed by my father and certainly by piano inventor Bartololmeo Christofori...

> you strike a key
> then a cluster for daylight
> as drunk as a lord

Jokerman

72

SIX OF CLUBS:
Key words: trustworthy – just – humour – gypsy.

Dear Six of Clubs,
the Pyramids are as fascinating as they are breathtaking. To visit Egypt was always in your mind. I know your nostalgia, your memories about Buddha sculptures, Gypsy music and Italian ceramic work. You dance the flamenco until your legs refuse. Manitas de Plata, rumba de los Cinco, the delicious perfume of your paella.

> *a moustache*
> *of chocolate milk*
> *your first party*

Seriousness can be the leading cause of everything, from dehydration to reincarnation. I don't observe your reflection with anxiety. You add a lot of humour into your life. Without action, no satisfaction! Smile and be happy. You told me once to involve my clown-chakra, a hot energy point located between our big toes and our earlobes. Indeed, he is indispensable and wonderful. To put this chakra into action we need only a good wine and a small bed. Or a banana on our head. As a crown on our crown?

> *under her photo*
> *a few rose petals*
> *and some butts*

Jokerman
in loving memory to Claire Buysschaert, mother of Hans & Saskia.

SEVEN OF CLUBS:
Key words: plucky – quiet – popular – visionary.

Dear Seven of Clubs,
your drawings are wonderful. I am afraid I do not express my feelings as clearly as you do yours, that can causes confusion for which I apologize. I feel the Zen of your ink an paper drawings, I don't lose sight on the purpose of your art: to rich inner freedom. Your art work express lightheartedness and satisfaction. You are painting young girls returning from bathing in the river.

> *blossoms*
> *after the rainfall*
> *brushstrokes*

Talking of writing and painting, loving what is beautiful, focused on study and mental exertions. Nothing is ever lost, you don't need your pencils or your brushes. I talk with sinners and saints, with skaters and peace activists. They all belong to one oceanic whole. They are our swinging brothers and good-natured sisters. You look at me and grin from ear to ear: 'They are all sincere but not serious.' I agree and call the waiter. One for the road!

> *tight as a drum*
> *sleeping under the table*
> *Happy New Year*

Jokerman

EIGHT OF CLUBS:
Key words: active – emotional – enjoyment – understanding.

Dear Eight of Clubs,
we don't lose our connection with nature. We are walking the descending and wooded slopes. The trees, glowing red and golden brown, are sacred. Autumn is gathering leaves, water is running fast in brooklets. Smell the ferns of our childhood. Remember the distant call of the tawny owls at night, feel the emotion you felt when you saw for the first time a sparkling hummingbird with hovering wings flying backwards. A greenish blue jewel hanging in place, at eye level. Do you also remember the fast shek-shek-shek of the Blue Jay sipping water on the small fountain at Bryce Canyon?

clear water
no more crayfish
only my big toe

Going back in time, sitting at the centre of a stone circle, you can see Orion's belt tonight. I move my outstretched arms, flap my wings and go for a round trip over the fruitful fields of wheat. I follow the ploughed land on both sides of the canals; enjoying the gaggling of the wild geese flying in an agile V-formation. I see dolphins foraging in the coastal waters and the mangrove rivers. Follow me.

in a reedy lake
a sudden rifle shot
the rattle of wings

Jokerman

NINE OF CLUBS:
Key words: spontaneous – watchful – grateful – winning.

Dear Nine of Clubs,
tune yourself with new sounds, united with the rituals of all times. Your name is freedom. Let playfulness liberate you. Discover new forces in meditation and singing. Blow your didgeridoo. Be a magician, taste inner relaxation through music. I am composing and dancing. The intended purpose is not the research for banal sensation or occult nonsense. White nor black magic, angels nor devils are under discussion. Smell the garden mould.

springtime
the keen cutting
of hedge shears

Give us a little bit more creativity and confidence. The study of ancient ceremonial rites is not really intended. Be welcome in the wondrous world of simple and beautiful sounds hovering in overtones and undertones. Leave the world of noise, contemplate about peace and commotion. Use meditation to improve health, self-esteem and creativity. Develop your own powers. Relativism and humour goes together. You are, just like me, a child of the eternal sounds. Walk in my garden, taste a strawberry.

motionless
on the garden gnome
a sparrow

Jokerman

TEN OF CLUBS:
Key words: globetrotter – teacher – loving – spicy.

Dear Ten of Clubs,
you are a passionated globetrotter. Go on exploration from metropolis to metropolis, always with your positive mental attitude. I see you walking, hand in hand with Nunguda the Masai woman. United colours. I see you as a horsewoman in Mongolia and taken by helicopter above the Grand Canyon. You reach the Kilimanjaro top, write love letters and teach the children, enjoying your Punch-and-Judy show about birds and butterflies. You know the monsoon forests and the harmony of the rice fields. Dry and wet seasons are your friends.

> on a wild river
> a rafting expedition
> lit up with joy

You visit the changing world of Mongolian's nomads, their ger, horses and lamas. You observe how they milk the mare, load the camels, erect prayer flags and wrestle with yaks and each other. In Bhutan you meet monks, wearing terrifying masks, in ritual dances rattling peculiar double-faced drums. A pilgrimage to the cavern of Amarnth or the streets of Paris? There you go, swinging along.

> old music
> and pancakes
> welcome in Bruges

Jokerman
to my beloved darling Jenny

JACK OF CLUBS:
Key words: justice – strong – inquiring – proud.

Dear Jack of Clubs,
you move quick as lightning on the spur of the moment. Talking with drag queens passing through, hip-hop dancing with nomadic people or running round all day with children and senior citizens. There you go again, fireproof, without bounds or restrictions. Running fast, you've been in tighter spots! Love is a consuming passion? Animal rights are important, so you act and react. Play the sax, contemplate the man leaning against the juke-box.

> nocturnal hour
> with a far-away look
> gazing the moon

Yielding, softness and centeredness are present. You are not afraid. The white crane spreads his wings and speaks against killing, sparing all lives. But what with killing time and poetry? For good reasons it is excellent to protect animals, like you and me, mammals with guns, destroyers with greed. Walk up and down the street, allow your eyes to see more. We can organize an African safari, control the Chinese civil rights or create a better road map for Israel. Peace will come.

> traveling people
> on different directions
> the same way

Jokerman
dedicated to my daughter Saskia & my son Merlijn

78

QUEEN OF CLUBS:
Key words: tenacious – temperament – hot – beaming.

 Q

Dear Queen of Clubs,
my first subway ride was in London on 24 May 1974, the day 'Duke' died. I still remember the double deck busses, a flock of geese around the Tower. I saw flightless ravens and your red dancing shoes. I heard a virtuoso performance on bass in the smoke-stained Marquee Club. Now, you are lighting a candle in Paris. I look around on the graveyard of Pere Lachaise, a cat sits on a funeral urn. In the distance an ambulance. We shelter from the rain under a fan vaulting. A family grave as umbrella. Trees invite to muse on Hanami.

> *our mortality*
> *gazing the blossoms*
> *set you thinking*

Hanami, a Japanese ritual in old times, was the most important festival leading to a good harvest. Farmers went out to see the wild cherry trees in the local forest to get a hint at when to start preparing the fields for the rice and how the harvest would be. Memories. We wrote a modest poetry book in our youth, with elements as a pagoda, bamboo flutes and a koto. Now I add more blossoms and a new springtime.

> *morning dew*
> *not one branche*
> *being hurt*

Jokerman

KING OF CLUBS:
Key words: ad rem – exuberant – gallant – powerful.

Dear King of Clubs,
dear sphinx. I am reading your story as a mysterious and magical cat, a powerful human-headed lion. I discover all the fascinating details of your being. They wake up my memories, there I go again for a haibun journey through New York, Nantes and Kathmandu. I am in tune with my own wants and needs. I believe in an upward spiral of knowledge-seeking. What makes the rivers flow and what the water rising? Who can tell me if the sea is running high?

> *in the shadow*
> *of the swelling waves*
> *just another wave*

The dunes are waiting with marram grass and firethorn. See the kaleidoscope of colours. Mind you for barbed wire. No man's land gathers footprints and desires. O, your salty kisses. I get quickly undressed to please you my lovely temptress. How does your hand find itself here? We are pounding away, murmuring old secrets of the sea.

> *a kiss on the beach*
> *she drapes a towel*
> *over his belly*

Jokerman

THE JOKER:
Key words: independent – fearless – unorthodox – gypsy.

Dear Joker,
i have your picture in my heart, mind and soul. Americans invented you around 1870, as the 'best bower,' the highest card in the game of Euchre. Dear joker, you became the trump card for that game. You know a lot about foolish pranks, and crazy farces? Put your fool's cap on, as nutty as a fruitcake, because you are familiar with our playful world. I observe your communal living with twinkling eyes and an independent mind with plenty of wisdom. A seer or a scatterbrain? There are all kinds of rumours going around:' Watch the joker, his foolishness is not what it seems to be. You are not the prodigal son, nothing gets lost. Be careful, certainly for yourself because life will throw you by incomprehension, as a chameleon, in at the deep end.

jokerman
living as a hermit
dreaming of toys

Jokerman

JOKER 2:
Key words: nature – sjamanistic – philosopher – hermit.

Dear joker,
you are a 'wildcard'! You do not belong to any of the suits. In some games, you are given by the holder any possible value... No problem, your intuition works faultless. You have no Herculean strength but you can make others look the fool. You take them for a ride, run the show and get a taste of your own medicine. You are the symbol of one of those people who get out and about as a playful child. I am permeated by your perfume and your cosmic forces. Sometimes you will fall head over heels in love. You are an excellent tightrope walker between firm intentions and shadows of doubt. You are laughing as a royal freebooter, heavenly mad in amazement. Sometimes a bad mood wins, however your initiation is those of a court jester: sheer folly gives birth to profundities.

playful jokerman
sing a last lullaby
for an old chap

Jokerman

MARIA STOVE'S CARD CLUB:

bridge club
she disrupts the silence
one beer please

on the sideboard
the winners and losers
so many photos

she wins
with the queen of clubs
storm in the air

sexy sax
there's a good mood
in a sultry dance

Bach or Zappa
that makes no difference
he plays bridge

reading about
serious bridge players
years gone by

playing cards
lost in daydreams
outside the snow

on his coffin
a few arum lilies
and the ace of hearts

on a rainy day
playing with pin-up cards
patience

worldwide
joker collectors
caps and bells

sweetheart
make hearts trumps
I am game

your eyes
lit up with joy
wich suit is trumps

a good game
and her children
trump cards

playing cards
and the value of simplicity
the scent of mint

in the shadow
of a black bamboo
playing solitaire

on the back
of his playing cards
sea cucumbers   *for robin d. gill*

awareness
beyond playing cards
her memories

siesta
a deck of cards
on her belly

the widow knows
a dozen variations
of solitaire

boarding
with a deck of cards
and his sadness

bloody hot
a knave of spades
in the pool

after the funeral
behind closed doors
the club members

modern times
playing cards and porno
on his laptop

her cards
in the strawberry bed
one gust of wind

a lot of fun
playing cards with unknowns
at the airport

at the wedding party
boredom on his face
no playing cards

my sweetie pie
is a good loser
strip poker

in the shadow
of the apple trees
playing trumps

hilarity
he declares trumps
drunk as a lord

he bluffs
with a good hand
froth in his moustache

she walks around
among the card players
her skirt with a slit

in the orchard
a bridge tournament
delicious smells

between the glasses
an old pack of cards
and your bra

an empty barrel
all the trumps are drawn
dim the lights

his leading card
and the waitress
pretty women

A REFLECTION:
(dedicated to Wim)

I have a rest in my hammock, between the carport and a mature quince. I am reading a smart reflection of my dear haiku-sister Jane Reichhold: 'The fact that the smallest literary form - haiku - has the most rules never ceases to amaze and astound. The only real comfort one can find in this situation is the concept that this affords a wider range of rules from which a writer can pick and choose. You cannot follow all of the rules and several of them are so contradictory that there is no way to honour them both at once. You must always choose. In order to make a choice, you have to understand the reasons and methods...'

Reasons and methods? Can my and your writing haiku be so rational-minded, so logical? I take a sip of my bourbon, scratch my head and peer at the empty sky. Reasons? I follow my heart. I write, a blind man may sometimes catch the crow...
I write a first sentence, a description of a feeling or an observation in a few words. A new line flows... now my pen's acting up. Three lines must talk straightforward, my mind stands aloof from thinking. A haiku linked with automatic writing? Oh dear...should I speak in tongues? Haiku and reasons: for what reasons? I prefer seasons.

As a freethinker I do not believe that we can have any smart opinion about what is told to be greater than our comprehension. My little 'cauliflower' is too small for such intricate stuff! So don't ask me to explain or follow gods & masters. I reject small talk about angels, heaven, sinners, senses of guilt or holy commandments. I believe in a free mind, not in proselytization. Graucho Marx once said: 'I don't want to belong to any club that will accept me as a member!' Great! But, I must admit that I pay a membership fee for a few haiku clubs: in Flanders, France, Japan and Australia...of course only to impress my old aunt and her Siamese cat.

Don't ask me why I started writing haiku, I don't know! Must there be any reason? Maybe because I was in search for an opportunity to combine poetry with an awareness of the world and myself. Maybe because I am inquisitive? I re-start every day! My first modest haiku was written in May 1968, this attempt enriched my whole life. Since a few years, haiku writing is a daily activity. Reading, study and writing in a close consideration with other kuyu learns that I still have the 'beginners' mind. To be on the lookout for new approaches is wonderful. It develops modesty and the ability to put myself, my haiku and the haiku rules in perspective. Geert in wonderland!

I love the discipline of daily writing. I try to write in several languages (Dutch, English, French and modestly in German), they have their own rules and habits to make an original contribution to the haiku world. It's a pity that I don't understand Japanese... to read Shiki and other masters in their native language. I translate my own Dutch haiku into English and French, and a few of them in German. People often get all in twist about how complicated translation is, how much is lost, how hard it is to convey the original. I go for it very straight, word-for-word with as little grammar or sentence structure as possible to be faithful to the original. I ask a few haiku poets to have a close look on the final result. With a little help from my friends...And: I accept a margin of errors, I am still learning by experience.

I write haiku in the most straightforward simple way as if I were a beginner! I don't try to make my haiku skilful, intellectual, smart or beautiful. I write haiku with full attention to discover the innocence of my first inquiry with an empty mind free of the habits of the so called experts. I try to see things as they are, in one flash. I face moment after moment and I forget all about rules and teachings...

A haiku is a thimble, which I try to fill up without spilling! Put briefly, haiku are objective, image-centered and 'one-breath' poems. I have a big mouth, so my haiku are rather short. It rarely happens that I submit my haiku to contests. To become famous or to be a haiku master is not my intended purpose. I am a modest haiku poet not a sneaky wrestler. I prefer to be a haiku poet without seeking chairmanship, medals of honour or golden cups. There are a lot of movements, schools and trends in the haiku world, with their own rules, customs, usages, practices, traditions and institutions. There are different clubs and associations, sometimes with conflicts of interests. They are recommended or heavily criticized...Who am I to judge? How can I judge?

There are a lot of opinions about the haiku world: it is a perfect mirror image of our society. Each opinion must be assessed on its own merits. Do I know the correct data and facts? Can I see the truth through dissenting opinions? I don't believe persistent rumours nor charges and accusations. If I cannot obtain correct answers, then I have to understand the questions. But I cannot read into the hearts of the critics living in different countries. And I refuse to show partiality. I refuse to accept forced convictions... so I prefer to write, read and study haiku without gossip factories or scoffing and abuse. I write haiku in the most straightforward simple way! I just write... with full attention and innocence, once in a while with an empty mind. Free of the habits of the so called experts. I try to see things as they are, in one flash. Facing moment after moment.

My favourite haiku-writers are, without any doubt: Masaoka Shiki (1867-1902) and the modern haikuists: Jack Kerouac, Gabriel Rosenstock, Lee Gurga, Jane Reichhold, Henk Werkhoven, Bill Higginson, George Swede, Robin d. Gill, Max Verhart... and many others. A basket of juicy fruits...just taste them.

Haiku is the poetry of experience, a perfect & peaceful way to exchange ideas and affirming the growing links among haiku poets around this blue planet. Methods? Ok, usually I am a methodical worker but do I use well-defined methods to write haiku? The rascal in me whispers: 'Not using methods is also a method.'

I take another sip. I am afraid that methodology is one of my weak points. It's a difficult problem, I admit. I am writing haiku, not compulsively, but I cannot give you a full explanation.

What is my aim? Burst upon the public, enter the public eye? No, I love my hammock... Underlying contrasts and contradictions are part of my game. Writing haiku can happen to the best of us. I close my eyes... and play solitaire.

HAIKU-QUOTES BY GEERT:

- 5-7-5 syllables? I try to be a haikuist, not an abacus!
- Haiku should be read in one breath, some people have rather small lungs...others a mouth big enough for two people.
- If a haiku is a temple, do you go inside to burn incense or to count syllables?
- A haiku is a miniature jewel case for daydreamers.
- A haiku is a four-star means against acidification.
- A haiku must be a thimble filled to overflow with emotion.
- Writing haiku is learning how to fly in the landscapes of your mind.
- Haiku have the colours of butterflies.
- Haiku are related to pebbles, not to armchair scholars.
- Haiku & whales, two mirrors for mankind.
- A haiku is a nutshell full of emotion.
- Even in a former life, I did not believe in reincarnation.
- As a freethinker I do not believe that we can have any smart opinion about what is told to be greater than our comprehension. My 'cauliflower' is too small for such intricate stuff!
- Don't ask me to follow gods nor haiku masters with small talk about senses of guilt or holy commandments and rules.
- Haiku and proselytization are conflicting. Writing haiku to promote religion or politics is nonsense.

GEERT VERBEKE

born 31 May 1948, in Kortrijk Flanders.
Children: Hans (1969), Saskia (1972), Merlijn (1984) & Jonas (1986). Haikuist since 1968. He survives excellently without membership cards or decorations. Free thinker & liberal, great supporter of the exchange of ideas between haiku poets writing in different languages. Recorded 11 cd's with singing bowls and world percussion

He writes: "Writing haiku and travel stories is where my heart lies. I prefer to write (Western) haiku, including both seasonal and non-seasonal poems. My life's pathway has taken various avenues including many `bread and butter' jobs: factory worker, service station attendant, artist, parks department worker, jazz-photographer, volunteer in terminal care & expert in Creative Problem-Solving (C.O.C.D, Antwerp).'
The focus of his haiku writing & singing bowls music is to strike a balance between structure and expression, between new creativity and amazement. He believes in the possibilities of haiku & music to promote a peaceful understanding and respect between people from all cultures.

His soulmate Jenny Ovaere, is a teacher and companion for Joker adventurous travelling. Jenny Ovaere is a teacher of mentally disabled youth. She serves as a travel companion for the Joker [Flanders] International Group Adventure Company and visits the places where she finds the subjects of her photography, which include Vietnam, Thailand, India, Mongolia and Nepal.
She writes: 'My passion for photography is a result of my travels around the world.' She also writes travel stories and creates necklaces.

HAIKU GEERT VERBEKE IN ANTHOLGIES:

EEN NIEUWE TAK: Haikoe-kern Antwerpen, 1990.
HET VOORJAAR KOMT PAS LATER: Concept 1993.
*HUIZEN IN AANBOUW:*Haikoe-kern Antwerpen, 1994.
DE EENHOORN SPRINGT WEER OP: Herkenrode 2002.
SCHADUW VAN REGEN: Haiku Kring Nederland 2002.
TWEE HALVE HARTEN: HKA, Antwerpen 2004.
*AAN HET WOORD:*De tuin van toen, Haikukring NL VL 2004.
TERPSCHICHORE: Lumière Poésie, Lille France, 2004.
THE ROAD, WORLD HAIKU: Bulgarian Haiku Club, 2004
EDITION WENDEPUNKT: Kalender, Weiden Duitsland 2005

HAIKU IN MAGAZINES & BOOKS:

GO-SHICHI-GO The Daily Yomiuri, Japan, April 2003.
AOZORA: International project South-east Europe.
WORLD TEMPOS JOURNAL: Japan, weekly haibun, 2003.
HAIKU REALITY: Srbia and Montenegro 2003.
GINYU MAGAZINE: N°18 & N°22, Japan: 2003 & 2004.
LYNX: A Journal for Linking Poets, June 2004, Jan. 2005.
GONG MAGAZINE: Nancy France: Juillet 2004.
LA REATA: East London, UK. Summer 2004
KLOSTRANSKI HAIKU SUSRETI ZBORNIK: Croatia 2004.
ALBATROS MAGAZINE 2004 N°1: Romania 02-11-04.
SIMPLY HAIKU: USA, Aug. 2003, 2004, Nov 2004.Feb 2005.
WORLD HAIKU WALL: NYC & Washington DC, 2004.
CHATS DU MONDE: Mudaison France, 2004.
LETNI ĈASI: Tevija Haiku Slovenije 2004.
CROATIAN HAIKU POETS: Poems of the month, 2004.
VUURSTEEN: Vlaanderen- Nederland, 2001 & 2004.
RAW NerVZ HAIKU, volume IX: Gatineau QC Canada 2004.
TAJ MAHAL REVIEW: Cyberwit's Journal,India 2004.
WORLD HAIKU, N°1: World Haiku Association, Japan 2005
FLY-KU!, book by Robin D. Gill: http://www.paraverse.org

SELECTIONS IN HAIKU-CONTESTS :

2nd WHA HAIGA CONTEST: Japan Mars 2003.
16nd WHA HAIGA CONTEST: Japan June 2004.
PRIX DE LION: Concours Montpelier, Frankrijk 2005
RUMOER IN DE LEESZAAL: Bibliotheek Turnhout, 2005.

HAIKU BOOKS:

HOOR HET MAANLICHT: reisverhalen met Jenny Ovaere.
KOKORO (E – FR – Dutch): Empty Sky editions 2004.
ADA: Photobook with Jenny Ovaere 2004.
RAIN: Published by Cyberwit, Allahabad India 2004.
VEGEN VAN REGEN: Haibun boek over dementie 2005.
CD 'ELEMENT' BY JOVICA STORER: Poland 2005.

REVIEWS:

KOKORO, Empty Sky editions, ISBN 90-805634-63:

Geert Verbeke describes haiku's nature in his book, 'The haiku shelters in moving emotion, in pure poetry and in what can not be explained'. Haiku's unique quality of capturing the essence of a moment and Geert's full spectrum style with distilled settings, whimsy, and profound insights brings to the senses the real charm of Nepal from the temples and the monasteries, to the streets, the markets, the people, and the land itself.
Poet Michael Baribeau, Michigan, USA.

With the news full of examples of atrocities, corruption, and killing, one needs, even more, to take in hand a book like Kokoro (Japanese for "heart"), go off to a quiet place and realize that there are good people and beautiful things on this earth if one just seeks them. Here is Geert Verbeke, a completely gentle soul who writes volumes of haiku (in both Dutch and English in this book), plays the Himalayan singing bowls (he has made ten CD's of his compositions), has written four books on the bowls (one published by Pilgrims' Bookhouse in Nepal).
Why can't the sonorous voices of newscaster teams discuss his work instead of yet another suicide bomber? His haiku have all the ·elements the news needs.

There is sadness:

grandpa is dying
the dense snowfall
covers his clogs

There is sex:

grandpa still looks
with lascivious glances
gran kisses his photo

There is madness:

for my grandfather
the moon is his daughter
each tree a son

And all of that on only one page of *Kokoro*. Each page has eight to eleven haiku so the reader gets a generous sampling of Geert Verbeke's many haiku. Though they are not divided into sections, the flow does move gently from one subject to another, from one experience into another – almost as one would watch a film.

Unhindered by the current emphasis in that corner of the world (Netherlands / Flanders) for strict 5 – 7 – 5 syllable count, Geert Verbeke's haiku have a natural rhythm and flow and perhaps you can see how exactly he translates the Dutch into English. Of all the Dutch haiku I've read, none sound as succinct and sweetly filled with life as his.

As far as I know this is the first time someone has issued a book of haiku and a matching CD. To sit and listen to the singing bowls is a great way to read the over 500 haiku in Geert Verbeke's book. The artwork throughout the book is simple but very effective in black, white and red. Here is someone doing everything to the very best of his ability to share the majesty and beauty in his life. All you have to do is to order the book and CD and there you have it!

I am very, very impressed with your work, I really love your haiku. And I do not say that often or lightly! You are very good- so good I find myself wishing I had written the haiku! Higher praise i can not give! **JANE REICHHOLD** in **LYNX,** A Journal for Linking Poets

ADA, Empty Sky edtions, ISBN 90-805634-71:
Together with his soulmate and life companion Jenny Ovaere, who provides the beautiful photographs for this book, Geert Verbeke set up in giving shape to that what ADA is. In his own way, using the three-line verses of haiku and the related senryū. The visual haiku as well as the narrative pictures are based on honest observations and concrete experiences. Coming from many a journey throughout their inner and outer worlds. They are nothing more than a reflection of their lovingly expression of life as it is.

Henk Werkhoven poet & musician, Apeldoorn the Netherlands.

I am enjoying reading your quirky haiku and looking at Jenny's colourful photographs. The two of them go together very well just as I imagine the two of you go together well. The book is beautifully designed and it's good to see the haiku in three languages, even though I can only read one of them. **Myron Lysenko, Brunswick Australia.**

RAIN, Cyberwit India, ISBN 81-8253-021-0:
Beautiful haiku with a strong figurative language, once in a while in a serious mood but for the most part cheerful, in a simple style. Geert has a grand mastership about all the subjects with a wide range of emotions. You can feel that the author feels at ease when he is writing, with attentiveness for the minutest details of life. The haiku is his view on the world. A book that I recommend. Geert has an open mind on the international society – he is a freethinker, pacifist, traveller, observer- his haiku are presented in English, French and Dutch. **Serge Tomé, for AFH Liège Belgium.**

Geert Verbeke's haiku, while written following the stringent guidelines of the most minimal haiku, have such a natural rhythm and flow, that the reader is unaware of the discipline to which he adheres. Due to the directness of his simplicity, he is then able to translate his haiku transparently into other languages. He is teaching us, not only how to write haiku, but also how to translate the poetry. Of all the Dutch haiku. I've read, none sound as succinct and sweetly filled with life as his.
Jane Reichhold, author of 'Writing and Enjoying Haiku,' USA 2005.

A FEW FOOTNOTES:

Balvenie: my favorite Single Malt Scotch Whisky.

Bashō: Matsuo Bashō (1644~1694) is known as the first great Japanese master in the history of haiku.

Bodhi Tree: at the western side of the Mahabodhi temple in Bodh Gaya (India), stands a large and historic Pipal Tree (ficus religiosa), known throughout history as the Bodhi Tree, under which Shakyamuni Buddha (Siddhartha), then known as Gautama, attained Enlightnment some 2500 years ago.

Ger: a portable dwelling used by the nomadic peoples of Mongolia.

Koi: a Japanese fish (Nishikigoi), developed over 200 years ago. The common carp is the forerunner of te Koi, they are not big godfisch. The goldfish is a distant cousin.

Narrow road to Oku: a haibun book of master Bashō, one of the highest attainments in the history of poetic diaries in Japan.

Playboy: magazine for study of nude rabbits.

Poe-tai Ho-Shang: Chinese zen-master.

Chris Rea: British singer-songwriter & guitarist, °4th March,1951.

Ryokan: Japanese monk teaching children, °Echigo, 1757.

Shakuhachi: an end-blown Japanese bamboo-flute.

Tsunami: a deadly sea wave.

Zen: (from Japanese,'zenna' or 'zenno' - from Chinese ch'an-na, or ch'an) a coalition of related ways for attaining realization, even beyond enlightenment, of the true nature underlying all appearances, including one's own-and above all, that there is no duality within appearances, but only the one buddha-nature.

Zen-Buddhism: culture of non -Being developed in the Far East. Developed in China (Chan Buddhism), and spread into Japan and Korea. It has incorporated several ideas from Taoism. Now spread in the whole world.